Self–Esteem for Women

BY EMILY HOSKINS

The Ultimate Women's Guide to Loving Yourself and Building High Self–Esteem

Third Edition

Emily Hoskins

© Copyright 2015 by Emily Hoskins- All rights reserved.

In no way is it legal to reproduce, duplicate, or transmit any part of this document in either electronic means or in printed format. Recording of this publication is strictly prohibited and any storage of this document is not allowed unless with written permission from the publisher. All rights reserved.

The information provided herein is stated to be truthful and consistent, in that any liability, in terms of inattention or otherwise, by any usage or abuse of any policies, processes, or directions contained within is the solitary and utter responsibility of the recipient reader. Under no circumstances will any legal responsibility or blame be held against the publisher for any reparation, damages, or monetary loss due to the information herein, either directly or indirectly.

Respective authors own all copyrights not held by the publisher.

Legal Notice

This ebook is copyright protected. This is only for personal use. You cannot amend, distribute, sell, use, quote or paraphrase any part or the content within this ebook without the consent of the author or copyright owner. Legal action will be pursued if this is breached.

Disclaimer Notice

Emily Hoskins

Please note the information contained within this document is for educational and entertainment purposes only. Every attempt has been made to provide accurate, up to date and reliable complete information. No warranties of any kind are expressed or implied. Readers acknowledge that the author is not engaging in the rendering of legal, financial, medical or professional advice.

By reading this document, the reader agrees that under no circumstances are we responsible for any losses, direct or indirect, which are incurred as a result of the use of information contained within this document, including, but not limited to, — errors, omissions, or inaccuracies.

Table of Contents

INTRODUCTION 7

CHAPTER 1: WHAT IS SELF-ESTEEM AND BODY IMAGE, AND WHY ARE THEY IMPORTANT? 9

CHAPTER 2: THE MEDIA'S INFLUENCE ON BODY IMAGE. 15

CHAPTER 3: IMPORTANCE OF HAVING HIGH SELF-ESTEEM 27

CHAPTER 4: DO YOU HAVE LOW SELF ESTEEM? 33

CHAPTER 5: HOW LOW SELF-ESTEEM CAN BE LINKED TO DEPRESSION 41

CHAPTER 6: HOW TO HAVE HIGH-SELF-ESTEEM 45

CHAPTER 7: STOP FALLING INTO THE COMPARISON TRAP 89

CHAPTER 8: HOW TO BOOST YOUR SELF-CONFIDENCE. 93

CHAPTER 9: HOW PRACTICING MEDITATION HELPS BUILD SELF-ESTEEM 103

CONCLUSION 113

Emily Hoskins

Introduction

I would like to thank you and congratulate you for downloading "***Self-Esteem for Women: The Ultimate Women's Guide to Loving Yourself and Building High Self-Esteem***".

Does any of this sound familiar? "I'm too tall." "I'm too short." "I'm too fat." "I'm too thin." "My nose is too big." "I hate my hair." "I wish I was prettier." "I'm not smart enough for the career of my dreams." "I will never find love." "If only I was smarter / more likable / taller / shorter/ thinner / curvier / had curly hair / straight hair / a smaller nose / a longer nose / longer legs / was more charismatic – then I'd be happy." These are the sounds of the all too familiar struggles, which nearly every woman has at some point experienced as a result of low self-esteem.

As women, we are often put under a tremendous amount of pressure to be perfect. Combined with the media's unattainable standards of "perfection", this can often leave us feeling insecure about ourselves, as well as cripple our self-esteem. This book is filled with valuable information and advice that will teach you and guide you on how to let go of the negative thought patterns that are associated with low self-esteem, and how to finally boost your level of confidence and self-esteem, while learning to love and appreciate yourself. This will help you improve many aspects of your life, including your relationships, career, the way others view you, and most importantly, your overall happiness and emotional well-being.

I trust my book will aid you on the path to improve your self-esteem and confidence. Enjoy your journey to self-acceptance and love. Remember—you're worth it!

Chapter 1

What is Self–Esteem and Body Image, and Why Are They Important?

Everyone has experienced self–esteem issues; it's just a normal part of being human. All sorts of people have had struggles with their self–esteem – including famously glamorous celebrities, and even flawless-looking supermodels who seemingly have ideal bodies. But what happens when low self–esteem begins causing problems in your family, work environment, relationships, and even your happiness and whole outlook on life? This book will help you identify your struggles with self–esteem, and will guide you on how to overcome low self–esteem. In time, you'll be able to appreciate the unique, beautiful person you are, inside and out!

You may have heard the words, "self–esteem" and "body image" before – but what do they mean?

Self esteem is the way you FEEL about yourself.
Body image the way you VIEW yourself physically.

What is Self–Esteem?

Self–esteem is all about the way you feel about yourself – how much you feel you are worth, and how much you feel other people value you.

Self–esteem is very important because it can play a huge part in your life by affecting your mental health, emotional well–being and overall outlook on your life. It also affects the way you behave when you're alone, as well as when around other people.

People with high self–esteem are realistic and know themselves well. They form positive relationships with people who treat them well and appreciate them for who they are. People with high self–esteem generally feel more in control of their lives, and also know their strengths and weaknesses, and have accepted them. People with high self–esteem are also more focused on the bigger picture in life, rather than constantly worrying about their personal insecurities.

What is Body Image?

Body image is the way you view your physical self – this includes whether you think you are attractive, and whether others think you are good–looking. Body image can be very closely linked to self–esteem.

Where Does Self–Esteem Come From?

Self–esteem isn't something we're born with. Self–esteem is something that gradually evolves throughout our lives as we develop and perceive an image of ourselves through the experiences in our lives with different people, situations and activities. Experiences during childhood particularly play a prominent role in the shaping of self–esteem. While we were growing up all of our experiences, including our successes, failures, and how we were treated by our family, teachers, religious authorities, coaches and peers, all played a significant role in the shaping of our self–esteem.

Self–esteem can be affected by a number of things, including poor health, life events associated with strongly negative emotions such as losing your job or getting divorced, unfulfilling or frustrating relationships, and a general sense of lack of control over your life. This can be sense of lack of control is namely marked in people who are the victims of emotional, physical, or sexual abuse, or are discriminated in regards to religion, culture, race, sex, or sexual orientation.

People who struggle with low self–esteem generally have the common tendency to see the world as a harsh, negative, hostile place and themselves as its victim. As a result, those with low self-esteem usually feel too insecure and reluctant to express and assert themselves. This causes them to miss out on many positive life experiences and opportunities, and feel helpless about making a change. As a result, their self-esteem becomes even further damaged, and they end up getting caught in a downward spiral.

One common thing that is often found in those with poor self-esteem is how they constantly rely on how they are doing in the present moment to determine how they feel about themselves. They typically have the constant urge to feed off positive external experiences – for example, compliments from their friends and authority figures to somehow create a balancing act, in attempt to eliminate the negative feelings and thoughts that constantly plague them throughout their everyday lives. However, even then, feeling good about themselves (after they've received a compliment/praise) is usually rather fleeing and temporary.

There are many different aspects that contribute to self-esteem, but according to clinical psychologist Dr. Lars Madsen it's often traced to abusive or dysfunctional early years, the effects of which can continue as the individual transitions into adulthood. It can also be the result of prolonged or ongoing stressful situation and life events, including relationship issues, problems with financial security, poor treatment/attitude from a partner, parent or guardian, being bullied, or being in either in a physically or emotionally abusive relationship.

Emily Hoskins

Chapter 2
The Media's Influence on Body Image

Many women struggle with their body image, which often contributes to low self-esteem. In fact, an astounding 10 million women in the UK are unhappy with their bodies. This is mainly because of the media's unattainable illusion of beauty standards.

Picking up a magazine or browsing through the internet can definitely trigger insecurities, as well as feelings of low self-esteem. This is because of how the media is flooded with photoshopped, airbrushed and unachievable images of the typical magazine cover "woman": a rail thin, six foot tall blonde woman with sky-high legs and large breasts.

After looking at these computer-enhanced photos, females immediately begin to develop a negative relationship with their bodies, and view themselves as grotesque, obese, and absolutely horrendous creatures, rather than the uniquely beautiful (and sexy!) women that they truly are.

Magazines have been using photoshop as a tool for a very long time to erase imperfections in celebrities and models. These "imperfections" include cellulite, stretch-marks, "inadequate" features such as legs that aren't long enough, and facial imperfections. For example, a photoshop experts will often make several computer-altered changes to a celebrity's face, such as slimming their nose, increasing the size of their lips and even changing the entire structure on their face!

Photoshop is also used to drastically alter the bodies belonging to the "perfect and flawlessly sexy" celebrities you constantly see on magazine covers. This computer program regularly "enhances" the bodies of the women on these magazine covers by cutting the width of their bodies in half, sometimes making them appear 30 pounds (about 2 stones!) thinner!

I used to constantly beat myself up over how there were so many attractive-looking women in the magazines I would read, who clearly had enough willpower to maintain such beautiful figures, and yet I couldn't discipline myself enough to look that way. After some time, it occurred to me that all of those gorgeous magazine women with seemingly perfect bodies did in fact have one thing in common, and no, it wasn't exceptional willpower. Their common "secret" was actually this slimming new technique called PHOTOSHOP!

With that said, it makes absolutely no sense to attempt to live up to these ridiculous standards while going through drastic measures, such as severely restricting your food intake and torturing yourself with excessive grueling sessions of exercise, when these are the "standards" of a computer.

The media does not only give us a false image of body shape, but also the idea that there is a "normalized" human body. The fact is, the human body is unique. There is no "right" way for the body to look. We're led to believe the female body should constantly be hairless, fit while remaining thin, with perfect make–up and hair no matter the situation. The fact is, no one wakes up in the morning with perfectly coiffed hair, with fresh, glowing skin. Similarly, no one is genetically inclined to flat abs and toned arms. Maintaining that illusion takes tremendous amounts of work and, usually, a team of people dedicated to making that person look good.

Celebrities utilize hair extensions, a make–up artists, expensive cosmetics, specially tailored clothing, and spa treatments. None of which is bad, or makes them less as a person, but it requires money and time that the average woman doesn't have available to her. Instead of trying to look like Scarlet Johansen, try to look like the best version of you. The best version of you is whatever you want it to be. Instead of focusing on wishing you looked like a celebrity or someone you know, focus instead of dressing and making yourself look like a version of yourself that makes you happy. Whether this involves dressing in cocktail dresses or yoga pants, wearing cat–eye eyeliner or no make -up, high heels or sneakers. Do what makes you happy. You're not obligated to look like anyone but you. As actress and comedian Amy Pohler is quoted as saying,

"We're all different, everybody's different, every body is different. There's only, like, five perfectly symmetrical people in the world, and they're all movie stars, and they should be, because their faces are very pleasing to look at, but the rest of us are just a jangle of stuff, and the earlier you learn that you should focus on what you have and not obsess about what you don't have, the happier you will be. You really will be happier in life if you let go of the things that you will never have."

Often, women trick themselves into thinking that if they make some major change to their body it'll finally bring them happiness. They go on fad diets that are ineffective and unhealthy, buy expensive new wardrobes, or get major cosmetic surgery. While this may be effective in some cases, often these women find themselves just as unhappy as they were previously. In this society we have access to more life–altering surgeries and cosmetics than ever before. While this is beneficial in some cases, the problem of unhappiness rarely stems from not being thin enough or having a large nose. It comes from low self–esteem. If you are unable to love yourself before undergoing a major physical change, it's unlikely you'll suddenly find the self–love you're craving. Which isn't to say making changes to try and find happiness is bad––no one should ever have to feel stuck in a situation they dislike. Still, it's important to learn to like yourself before seeking out happiness through drastic physical change. You may not be the ideal weight now or your breasts may not be the size you want them to be, but taking the time to develop a healthy relationship with yourself is the first step to higher self–esteem and, ultimately, happiness.

We often feel trapped in our body, especially if it limits what you're able to do. Your body may not look the way you think a healthy body looks, but take a moment to appreciate what it can do. If you are able–bodied, rather than focusing on the cellulite on your thighs, appreciate that your legs are strong enough to carry you from one place to another. Your arms might be strong enough to push a wheelchair or carry a toddler up a flight of stairs. Your stomach may have stretch marks from having a child. Your body, whatever it looks like, is the story of your life. Don't be ashamed of its imperfections—everyone has them, and yours are unique to the life you've lived so far. The human body is an amazing feat of engineering, no matter what its condition is. You have the capacity to be and do whatever it is you wish to. When we put ourselves down and compare our bodies to others we forget that our very existence is something to celebrate.

Small changes to our life can often make us feel better when we find ourselves falling into a rut. Eat foods that make you happy. If you're happiest when following a strict dietary plan, then make one out for yourself. If you find yourself happiest when you eat things that make you feel good, balance that out. Don't give up pizza and cake, but eat fresh vegetables and fruits. Find an activity that you enjoy and do it as often as you can. Take walks in your favorite place where you live or work. Do yoga or other stretching while watching your favorite TV show. Go for a swim, or take a boxing class. Try to dress with how you feel in mind. Maybe sweat pants and a t-shirt are the simplest things to put on in the morning, but think about how that makes you feel. If it makes you feel good, then continue doing it. But if it makes you feel bad, find little ways to change that. Buy a shimmery new eye shadow or a comfortable pair of jeans that make you feel good about your shape. Remember, you have the capacity to be happy being you. Once you stop comparing your looks to others, you have the ability to find what makes you feel like you.

Sometimes it's helpful to find a positive comparison. Maybe you're feeling down about your body. You dislike how thin it is, or the way your stomach hangs. Rather than focusing on a celebrity with a body shape that is unobtainable to you, try to find some inspiration in someone with a similar shape. Look at photos of Amber Riley, Rebel Wilson, or Mindy Kaling, all of whom are stunning. They're are models like the beautiful Jillian Mercado, who has muscular dystrophy. There are less contemporary role models like Frida Kahlo. If you try to find someone with a similar body and can't, know that this is the media's fault, and not yours. You are not culpable for the lack of representation in movies and media.

Finally, sometimes it's necessary to accept what we view as "flaws" about ourselves. Maybe you dislike your lips, or think you have too much body hair, or that your skin isn't clear enough. Take a moment every day to appreciate the parts of you you're most insecure about. Tell yourself you love your nose when you look at the mirror. Sit down, close your eyes, and take a moment to touch and appreciate the parts of your body you're most insecure about. Instead of avoiding the things that you dislike about yourself, face them head–on. Maybe you'll never learn to truly appreciate them, but you can teach yourself to stop beating yourself up over them. Remember, your flaws are what make you unique!

Sometimes it's helpful to remember that the way you look at yourself is often vastly different than the way others view you. You probably focus on flaws that others don't even see. The things you find enviable in others may be what they consider "flaws". It's not unlikely that others find many enviable things about your appearance!

It's not wrong to want to better yourself, but making sure that you're good to yourself should always be your main priority. Remember, you deserve love and respect in all aspects of your life, and your body is no different.

#1 **BODY IMAGE RULE**:

Do not (under any circumstances!) compare yourself to any image presented to you by the photoshopped entertainment industry. Most of the photos you see in magazines have been touched up in one way or another – ESPECIALLY magazine covers!

I recently came across several before and after photos of various photoshopped celebrities. I was shocked to see how much of a difference there was between the two photos – in some cases, the celebrities were completely unrecognizable. Every inch of their bodies seemed to be photoshopped. In fact, the "before" pictures showed that these seemingly perfect-looking, flawless glamazons actually looked like completely normal women without the shape-shifting photoshop alterations.

DISTORTED BODY IMAGE: EATING DISORDERS

The media's negative influence on our bodies can leave many women with a distorted body image. This can lead them into developing an eating disorder, which is a very serious physical and psychological illness.

There are 3 types of eating disorders: Anorexia Nervosa, Bulimia Nervosa and Binge-Eating Disorder (BED).

ANOREXIA NERVOSA

Anorexia Nervosa is characterized by the incessant pursuit of thinness, as well as the intense fear of gaining weight. Women who suffer from anorexia have a distorted perception of their image. For example, a rail-thin young woman suffering from anorexia will see herself as overwcight. Anorexics severely restrict their caloric intake with severe dieting/fasting, and/or excessive exercise.

BULIMIA NERVOSA

Bulimia Nervosa is characterized by binging on extremely large quantities of food, followed by abusing laxatives and/or vomiting (purging) the large portion of food that was consumed to avoid weight gain. During their excessive binges, bulimics experience a loss of control. Examples of a bulimic's binge foods include a whole pint of ice cream, an entire container of cookies or pastries, or a whole bag of crisps, consumed over a very short period of time.

BINGE EATING DISORDER (BED)

This more recently studied disorder is similar to bulimia with its binging characteristics, although it doesn't involve purging. People who suffer from binge eating disorder (BED) periodically binge on immensely large qualities of food, although they do not vomit or abuse laxatives afterwards, like those with bulimia do.

These are all very serious disorders that can greatly effect health, as well as crush self-esteem even further.

This is why it's important to use positive strategies when trying to lose weight. Always remember, NOBODY IS PERFECT! You don't have to be a stick–thin to be beautiful. In fact, despite the media's totally unrealistic false standards of "beauty." Women come in all shapes and sizes, not one of which is more beautiful than the others.

However, if you are trying to shed a few pounds, make this happen with healthy lifestyle choices, such as eating healthier foods and including exercise in your weekly routine. This will be much more effective than a ridiculous "starve yourself" diet fad.

Always remember that you are a uniquely created, beautiful individual, and that the universe would not have you any other way!

Emily Hoskins

Chapter 3
Importance of Having High Self–Esteem

Having high self–esteem is important namely because it is essential for getting the most out of your life's journey and experiences. Here are some of the amazing impacts high self–esteem has on your life:

Life becomes simpler, lighter and significantly less stressful

When you learn to love and appreciate yourself more, life becomes much easier. This is because you won't be so hard on yourself or beat yourself up so much over simple mistakes that fall short of your unrealistically perfect standards.

Something that may strike you about confident people is that they don't seem as burdened with the little nuisances of everyday life. They're able to shrug off inconveniences and set–backs much easier than those with low self–esteem, who may take these moments too much to heart. Try not to focus too much energy on the small stuff––at the end of the day, you're life is what you make, and it becomes significantly less burdened when we don't hold onto the little negative parts of our day.

Emotional vulnerability is replaced with inner stability

When you develop high self–esteem, you no longer worry so much about what others may think of you. This is because you already have a high opinion of yourself, and don't need to seek attention from others to feel valued. You also become less needy in your personal life, and lose the tendency to go on emotional roller coasters based on what others may think of you.

It may seem daunting, but it's important to remember that the only opinion that matters is your own. Others may judge you for living your life a certain way, or for choosing to look one way, but at the end of the day their opinions, good or negative, won't make you happy. Often, we seek gratification from others to feel good about ourselves, but even ego boosts are temporary. By loving ourselves, we hold the key to do what we want and to be ourselves without worrying about the opinions of others. Not only will it boost your confidence and self-image, but it will make it easier for you to make friends and other important connections. It may also prove helpful to achieving your goals. Those who don't believe in themselves often are unable to get what they want out of life.

You will have better friendships and relationships

When you have high self-esteem, it becomes much easier to maintain strong relationships because being around you is a lighter experience, and doesn't come with constant drama, tension, fighting and arguments that are based on little to nothing. You view things in a more positive way, and are more focused on life's bigger picture, as well as the broader scheme of things, rather than pointless negativity-fueled drama. You also become more giving, and a better listener. These are all highly-respected and attractive traits seen in a relationship, as well as a platonic friendship.

While it's important to surround yourself with people who make you feel good about yourself, relying on others to aid in your emotional health and self-confidence all the time can be very draining for them. We all like to be reminded that we're worth the time of others, but when our self–esteem tends to be low we can find ourselves in a place where we require constant reassurance from others. By improving your self–esteem, your friends and loved ones will be able to focus a place where we require constant reassurance from others. By improving your self–esteem, your friends and loved ones will be able to focus on you and you'll be able to focus on them, without any of the complications that can result from self–esteem issues getting in the way.

Less self–sabotage

People with low self–esteem are often their own worst enemy. They are constantly sabotaging themselves, and setting themselves up for failure. This is because they don't feel like they deserve the better things in life, and subconsciously work against themselves rather than making efforts to set up goals and succeed in life. On the other hand, people with high self–esteem feel more deserving of the good things in life, and pursue their goals with more motivation because they feel they are worth it.

When you feel confident with yourself, you'll find that you're able and willing to experience new things. You'll gradually find yourself worrying less and less about what others think as your confidence and self-esteem grow. Those who are truly confident don't worry about looking like a fool——they allow themselves to live life to the fullest. It may be easier to approach romantic partners, make new friends, or enjoy time with the people who are currently in your life. Think of something you enjoy, but are too self-conscious to engage in. Maybe you love dancing, but worry too much that you're a bad dancer. Maybe you enjoy singing, but think no one will want to hear your voice. You may even feel like you have to feel shameful for the television shows you watch or a hobby you participate in. Whatever it is, know that the opinions of others don't dictate what you do in life. If it makes you happy, go for it! Once you feel good about yourself, you'll no longer restrain yourself from having fun.

You will be happier

As mentioned earlier, the key to happiness often lies with ourselves. With confidence and high self-esteem, you'll trust yourself to make necessary changes to improve your overall quality of life. Go for your dreams!

Emily Hoskins

The only thing keeping you from living the life you want is yourself!

Chapter 4
Do You Have Low Self–Esteem?

Low self–esteem usually results from deep–rooted childhood experiences. For example, if a parent mistreats a child, the child will believe they deserve it, and if a parent abandons a child, the child will see view themselves as insignificant. If a parent withholds love and affection, the child will automatically deem themselves unlovable. As they grow older, they subconsciously continue holding onto these beliefs that they were molded in, and see themselves through unrealistically negative and distorted lenses, and generally assume that people see them in the same negative way they view themselves, which of course translates to low self–esteem.

However, there are other factors that can play into the development of low self–esteem. Being bullied as a child by classmates at an early age can also contribute. A child who is berated by her peers for being fat, for example, may develop a negative relationship with her body. If a young girl is ostracized from the other girls in her class, she might think she is not worthy of love.

Similarly, low self–esteem can develop from abusive relationships with partners or friends. We've all had "toxic people" in our lives at one point or another, and often these people prey on those they perceive as not being confident. They may constantly tell their partner, "No one else will ever love you", or criticize her appearance or hobbies. A common tactic with abusers is to make their loved one feel useless and unlovable in an attempt to gain control of them. This can greatly increase low self–esteem and form a deep–rooted dislike of one self, even if the abusive relationship has ended.

These are, of course, just a few examples of where self–esteem issues stem from. You may find some of these situations familiar, or you may not. It can be incredibly helpful to deeply reflect and try to uncover the exact source of your low self–esteem. Sometimes it can feel painful to think back to times when we were mistreated, like opening an old wound, but your low self–esteem is the result of the wound never healing properly. You can't break a bone and leave it without medical attention in hopes that it'll be good as new. Instead, the bone needs to be set. Your low self–esteem is like a bone that healed the wrong way––the wound is no longer fresh, but it will continue to give you trouble until it is taken care of properly. Once you are aware of where it is coming from, you can begin to heal.

COMMON CHARACTERISTICS OF PEOPLE WITH LOW SELF–ESTEEM:

Irrational and Distorted Inner Self Statements

People with low self–esteem carry on an inner dialogue with themselves in which they make untrue or unproven statements about themselves. They will also inwardly agree with the negative feedback of others, even if they initially choose to argue against the criticism.

A person with low self–esteem may think to themselves, "I'll never be good enough" or "I can't change my situation." Their self–esteem may not even be linked to their physical appearance, but an overall sense of inadequacy. It may keep her from applying to a job, asking a love interest out, or reaching out to make a friend. Low self–esteem can be debilitating and prevent development.

Generally not confident that they will succeed in life

When something discouraging happens, people with low self-esteem will view the situation as an indication that they will never prevail in life. Even overachievers with low self-esteem share a similar thought pattern, as they hold a belief that their success will eventually evaporate.

Any success achieved may feel short lived. Those with low self-esteem will undercut their achievements with statements like, "I could have done better" or "It's not a big deal". They often view their success as something anyone could accomplish. When they are not successful, they are much harder on themselves than they need to be.

Prone to obsessive-compulsive or addictive behaviors

People with self-esteem will often attempt to make themselves feel better by becoming involved in over-spending, overeating, alcohol-use, perfectionism, drug use and sexual promiscuity. These behaviors can often become unhealthy, and in some cases, dangerous, life-threatening addictions.

Overreact or become easily offended in situations where others do not

Filled with negative thoughts about themselves, those with low self-esteem are generally prone to emotionally overreact in situations in which a person with healthy self-esteem would not. For example, they may overreact at a comment they feel is offensive or inappropriate.

They may also take things more personally than others might. While someone with healthy self-esteem may be able to remove themselves from a situation and see that the result of something is circumstantial, a person with low self-esteem may take the actions and words of others as a criticism of themselves. It can lead to irrational outbursts and unnecessary arguments that can strain relationships.

Indecisive

People with low self-esteem have a very difficult time in making decisions – even when it comes to small, insignificant things, like what they're going to wear that day. This is because people with low self-esteem are extremely concerned (and in some cases obsessed) with what others think of them, and how they perceive them. That being said, simple actions like getting dressed for the day can often be very stressful and demanding tasks for those with low self-esteem.

Experience a great deal of shame

People with low self-esteem often feel a great deal of shame from past and present situations. Instead of lightheartedly laughing off an embarrassing situation and moving on, people with low self-esteem continuously beat themselves up over something embarrassing they experienced, and feel immensely shameful about it for extended periods of time.

They may not be able to let go of past experiences, no matter how inconsequential. They may go over the same conversation over and over again, thinking of what they should have said. They may return mentally to something that has happened many years in the past and regret their decisions. They may lie awake at night, unable to sleep, worrying about the past. For example, a waitress might say to you, "Have a nice meal", after serving food. You may respond, "You too". It's a silly little mistake that everyone makes at some point, but someone suffering from intense low self-esteem may feel excessively embarrassed by the event. They may worry that the waitress thinks they're stupid. Instead of letting the mishap go, they might bring it up to the waitress, who likely forgot it ever occurred.

Constant worrying about the future

Those with low self–esteem live in constant worry and fear over what the future may bring. They don't believe they have what it takes to establish a promising future for themselves.

Similarly, this can affect sleep and make their own head a difficult one to inhabit. They may worry that they will never be good enough to obtain any of their goals or to proceed in life. They might be concerned that they'll always be alone or that their family and friends will leave them. They might also be concerned about being in poverty or not being able to afford medical expenses should the need arise.

Emily Hoskins

Chapter 5
How Low Self–Esteem Can Be Linked to Depression

Low self–esteem and depression have a big thing in common – they both fill a person's mind with negative thoughts. The way you perceive yourself forms your self–esteem either positively or negatively. Negative experiences are big contributors to this, as they greatly influence the low self–esteem someone develops. Depression, on the other hand, is a psychological and physical disorder – as it can manifest physically after a period of time – that stems from within, but can very often be influenced by self–esteem.

Researchers have found many connections between low self–esteem and depression, and have discovered that people with low self–esteem have an significantly increased risk of falling into depression. However, if those with low self–esteem can be immediately treated before their poor self-esteem progresses into depression, then they may avoid falling into the grip of depression later on.

Julia Friederike Sowislo, a Swiss researcher of the Department of Psychology at the University of Basel, has recently evaluated the unique relationships between low self-esteem, depression, and anxiety. Sowislo researched 95 separate reviews that involved participants of all different ages and various backgrounds.

Sowislo found that low self-esteem could, in fact, increase the frequency and intensity of depression and anxiety.

You may already be familiar with depression. Do you ever feel like even the simplest task is impossible to do? Do you find yourself listless, unable to gather energy for anything, and wishing you could spend the entire day in bed? Many people associate depression with a deep sadness, and while that may be the case, often it's an absence of emotion. Depression acts as a blackhole that sucks in everything good about your life and making it seem like there isn't a point in living. You may no longer be grooming yourself, cleaning your home, or responding to friends. Alternatively, you may find yourself much more irritable than what is considered "normal" for you.

When low self–esteem and depression are combined, the result is a vicious cycle of helplessness and emotional instability. Depression can be extremely debilitating to someone in many ways. For example, it prevents someone from socializing, even when the person with poor self–esteem self is already angry with themselves for not having many friends.

When low self–esteem and depression are combined, the result is a vicious cycle of helplessness. Depression can be extremely debilitating and can prevent someone from socializing, even when the person with low self–esteem is already angry with themselves for not having many friends. In addition, both depression and low self–esteem are often related to eating disorders, as self–esteem causes distorted views of a normal body, leading the person to feel the need to lose weight to look more "attractive". If the person feels like they have failed, they may fall into depression. As a result, this may prevent them from finding the mental willpower, motivation and physical strength to work towards achieving their goals.

The highly detrimental problem with believing we're no good is that we start to behave and live as if it's true.

"Low self–esteem often changes people's behavior in ways that act to confirm the person isn't able to do things or isn't very good," says Chris Williams, Professor of Psychosocial Psychiatry at the University of Glasgow. "In the short term, avoiding challenging and difficult situations makes you feel a lot safer,"

Professor Williams explains, "In the longer term, this avoidance can actually backfire because it reinforces your underlying doubts and fears. It teaches you the unhelpful rule that the only way to cope is by avoiding things. You need to look at your beliefs, how you learned them and why you believe them. Then actively begin to gather and write down evidence that disconfirms them. Learn to spot the negative thoughts you have about yourself. You may tell yourself you are 'too stupid' to apply for a new job, for example, or that 'nobody cares' about you. Start to note these negative thoughts and write them down on a piece of paper or in a diary. Ask yourself when you first started to think these thoughts. It's about helping people recognize they have strengths as well as weaknesses, like everyone else, and begin to recognize those strengths in themselves. You might have low confidence now because of what happened when you were growing up. But we can grow and develop new ways of seeing ourselves at any age."

Chapter 6
How to Have High–Self–Esteem

As Viktor Frankl, a psychiatrist and Holocaust–survivor famously once said in his book, *Man's Search for Meaning*, "Everything can be taken from a man but one thing; the last of the human freedoms – to choose one's attitude in any given set of circumstances, to choose one's own way."

Although truly loving and appreciating yourself takes some time, there are many actions you can take that will help you develop much higher self–esteem. Here are some tips that will help you let go of the negative feelings of low self–worth, and replace them with high self–esteem, as well as a positive, self–respecting mindset.

1). LOSE THE PERFECTIONISM

Perfectionism is a very self–destructive thinking habit that can viciously sink your self–esteem, as well as your whole outlook on life.

People who have a perfectionist–mindset become paralyzed with fear at the thought of falling short of their unrealistic expectations. This often causes them to procrastinate on their goals and prevents them from taking action because they are terrified of being seen as "average".

Perfection is impossible – it's unachievable for any of us. So just let it go already! Get rid of that nagging pressure to be perfect! You're never, ever going to be perfect. No matter how hard you beat yourself up, you're never going to have the perfect body, the perfect life, the perfect career, the perfect relationship, the perfect children, or the perfect home. Life comes with ups and downs, and the downs are inevitable. This is something you will have to learn to accept. We are constantly dwelling with the idea of perfection, because we see so much of it (or rather, a staged, photoshopped, unrealistic illusion of perfection) in the media. Whatever seems perfect in the media is simply an artificial recreation of society. It doesn't exist.

Instead of grasping on your unattainable desire for perfection take account of your accomplishments as you achieve them. Acknowledge their actual value to yourself, rather than downplaying and de-valuing them by saying, "Oh, that? That was nothing compared to what could've been done by someone else. It's not special or a big deal." Keep a fun little journal (decorate it for some extra pizazz!) documented with a list of things you accomplish. This is an opportunity to make a reflection of yourself that you're happy to return to each day. You can buy a pretty journal from the store, or buy a blank one to decorate yourself. Don't feel obligated to limit yourself to words! You can add drawings, tickets stubs and other scrap paper that gives you good memories, or pictures you enjoy from the internet or magazines. Get creative! We often find an outlet for difficult feelings by channeling our creative side. And because the journal is for your eyes only, you don't have to worry about someone else judging it. If you dislike a page, you can merely never look at it again. When you find yourself making an accomplishment, add it to the journal of accomplishments! There are some people who even prefer to write on a daily basis, while others feel more comfortable just noting them every now and again – maybe once a week or a few times a month. The key idea here is to accomplish your smaller goals and little by little, move on from each small goal to the next, like a connect–the–dots game of life.

It's just as important to accept the mistakes you make in life, and take them as learning experiences that will help you grow. Making mistakes is normal – it's all part of being human, everyone does it. Making mistakes certainly doesn't indicate that you're a bad person or a failure – all it simply means is that you made a mistake (just like everyone does). Mistakes are an essentially part of life – they're opportunities for learning and for growth, allowing you to see what works and what doesn't. Instead of beating yourself up for every single little mistake, remove yourself from the pointless self–pity or negative self–talk, stop wallowing in misery and try and see it from someone else's point of view. Seeing it from another person's perspective will help you see how petty and insignificant your complaints and worries are. They're actually not a big deal!

Instead, aim for "good enough". When you are constantly determined to reach a level of perfection, this usually winds up unfinished tasks, projects and goals. Case in point, there is no such thing as the "perfect human", therefore it is impossible to always have the perfect results with everything. Replace the standard of "perfect" with the standard of "good enough", as this is much more realistic. This will help you be a lot more successful in effectively achieving goals.

2). HANDLE MISTAKES AND FAILURES IN A POSITIVE WAY

Instead of beating yourself over mistakes, find the upside in every situation. Always focus on being optimistic and seeing the opportunities you have in life. Whenever we step out of our comfort zone. We're bound to make mistakes before we finally get it right – and that's OK!

One of the most misleading ideas that we keep with us through life is that failure is a negative thing. The fear of failure often keeps us from trying new things, and often is a major cause of anxiety. In fact, failing in the past and being chastised for it may be one of the "sources" of your low self–esteem. Instead, think of failing as a magnificent learning opportunity. We all fail sometimes. It doesn't matter how gifted we are or how successful, failure is a necessary part of life. Without failure, we often don't have the push to better ourselves.

Some examples of successful women who have "failed":

Before becoming a talented television mogul and successful actress, Lucille Ball's first films failed. Critics referred to her as "the queen of B movies."

Oprah Winfrey grew up impoverished and was subject to awful abuse as a child. During her early career she was demoted news co–anchor to morning television where few viewers would watch. She is now known for her famous television talk show, her own network, and magazine.

JK Rowling's iconic Harry Potter series was rejected by dozens of publishers before finally being accepted. At the time of writing it, Rowling was a poor mother living off of government assistance.

Marilyn Monroe was initially told by casting agents to "try being a secretary" before making it as a successful pin–up model and actress.

Lady Gaga was dropped by a major record label after only 3 months on–board. She has since sold millions of records.

Emily Dickinson had only a handful of her poems published before her death. Now, her 1,800 existing poems are wildly celebrated by literary enthusiasts.

Frida Kahlo was in a horrific bus accident that left her barren and forced her to undergo more than 30 surgeries. Kahlo was in constant pain as a result, but still managed to create wonderful works of art and live a prolific life.

Had these women succeeded early on, who knows where they'd be today. Instead, these early failures shaped their determination that later led to success. While failure can be daunting and draining, it's important to move on and reflect on what you've learned from the experience. You can take something positive from just about every experience in your life. The only time you've truly failed is when you stop growing.

3). DON'T FALL VICTIM TO YOUR INNER CRITIC

Learn how to say "stop" to your inner critic. There is no need to be so impossibly hard on yourself!

While your inner critic can definitely motivate and push you to get off your bum, step forth and accomplish things in life, it can also drag down your self–esteem by causing you to be far too difficult on yourself.

When you hear your inner voice constantly nagging that you're not good enough, learn to say "no" to these thoughts, and replace them with more helpful and positive thoughts.

Negative Inner Critic:

"You are such a lazy, fat cow! I can't believe you only lost such a small amount of weight this month. You're such a failure."

Positive Frame of Thought:

"Although I didn't meet my ideal weight–loss expectation, I still put in effort and saw some results, which means my effort paid off to an extent! This week, I will try harder to exercise more often and eat more vegetables, so I can get to an even healthier weight.

If the critic is telling you something negative, feel free to talk back to it and yell "STOP!", or something more creative like, "We are not going there!", or "OVERULED!" Because YOU are the judge of your thoughts, NOT your inner critic!

A healthier frame of mind = less stress, less negativity, and a much happier you!

4). USE HEALTHIER FORMS OF MOTIVATION

Rather than trying to push yourself by accepting the negative thought patterns regarding your current self, use healthier motivational habits to meet your goals. Here are examples of positive self-motivation:

"By earning more money, I will finally be able to have my dream of traveling around the world with the love of my life."

"If I eat healthier and exercise more often, I will be in much better physical shape, and will have more energy to participate in activities with my kids. I will also improve my health, and will have a higher-quality lifestyle."

"If I practice painting, I will improve and can share my art with others."

Remember, being unnecessarily harsh on yourself will do nothing to make any positive life changes. Instead, encouraging yourself to live life to the fullest will allow you to make changes you want.

5). ACKNOWLEDGE WHAT YOU LIKE ABOUT YOURSELF

A highly beneficial way to boost your self-esteem is to turn your focus onto the things you like about yourself, rather than constantly dwelling on the negative aspects. Write down at least 5 things you like about yourself. This will allow you to open your eyes and cause you to realize that there is in fact a wonderful side to you! It will also help you significantly cut back on the criticism and negative self–talk.

Take those five things and repeat them to yourself in the mirror each morning. It may seem silly, but studies show that vocalizing the good qualities you posses increase your self–esteem. Begin each day by reminding yourself that you are loved and deserve to be loved. There's nothing wrong with being your own biggest fan! Practice saying phrases such as:

"I am beautiful. I'm lucky I get to look at myself every day."

"I am smart and competent. I am going to walk into the office with my head held high."

They may seem silly and boastful, but believing you're your own best friend is a key to successfully learning to love yourself.

If the self–critic seems to continue to dominate your inner–voice, give it a moment to speak its mind. Open a word document, or grab a pad of paper, and write it all down. Everything that comes to mind for ten minutes. It may surprise you how mean your inner–critic is. Would you ever say this to someone you cared about? If the answer is no, then realize you should not be thinking such things about yourself. Once that is done, start a new page. This time, write about yourself as if you were writing about your best friend. Focus on the things that you like about yourself. Go into great detail. Write about the exact hue of your eyes, or that time you stopped in traffic to help a stray dog find its home. Even if you have to fake liking things about yourself, find something to write about. Don't let any negativity creep in. Once you're finished, save the love letter and re-read it to yourself when you're feeling down about yourself. Remember what you like about yourself, and that those things haven't changed. Treating yourself well is the first step toward finding self-love.

6). SPEND YOUR TIME WITH UPLIFTING PEOPLE

An important way to develop high self-esteem is by spending time with positive people who uplift you and make you feel good about yourself, rather than with negative and condescending "toxic" people who constantly bring you down, and lower your self-esteem even further down. Eliminating the toxic people from your life and replacing them with kind, uplifting and positive people will immensely help you boost your self-esteem to a much healthier level.

It may be difficult to remove or distance yourself from toxic people. These people may be close friends, partners, or even family. You may try to convince yourself that their negative behavior isn't so bad ("Oh, she's only teasing me about my weight. It's only because she cares about me".), or that you're overreacting. The fact is, we all have negative people in our lives, and these people tend to prey on those with low self-esteem who are less likely to call-out the behavior. If it's possible, cut these people out of your life completely. The situation may become more difficult if it's a family member that you'll be forced to interact with at gatherings. It may be more effective to distance yourself from them and maintain limited contact. If you are in an abusive relationship, it may be helpful to contact a local women's shelter to exit the situation safely. We all deserve to be treated with love and compassion, and if you suspect that those around you are bringing you down, you have every right to remove them from your life. It doesn't matter how long you've known them or how they're connected to you.

7). USE POSITIVE AFFIRMATIONS

A great way to boost feelings of self-worth and make yourself feel significantly better about yourself is by telling yourself positive affirmations. Tell yourself things like, "I am a kind, hardworking and successful person", and "I am beautiful on the inside and out". If you start repeating these affirmations to yourself, it will begin making a very big difference over time.

As mentioned earlier, it may be helpful to focus on specific parts of yourself that you like at first. Maybe you dislike your body, but very much so enjoy a tattoo that you have on your arm. You can first start by reminding yourself that you like your tattoo--how colorful it is, what it means, the artistry behind it. After some time, you may be able to start looking at how it looks on the body part--the way it curves or lays flat, the way it looks on your skin. From there, you may be able to begin appreciating parts of your body that you otherwise dislike. Find the positive in your body. Enjoy the roundness of your stomach or the litheness of your limbs. Appreciate the stretch marks and cellulite as signs that you've lived. Typically, only children and fictional people are completely free of these markings. Even the celebrities who look spot-free on magazine covers (remember, photoshop).

8). THINK POSITIVELY ABOUT YOURSELF

When you find yourself beating yourself up, always remind yourself that despite your problems, and setbacks you may be experiencing, you are a unique, special, meaningful and valuable person, and that no matter what happens in your life, you deserve to feel good about yourself. Identify and speak against any negative thoughts that you may have about yourself, such as "I am a failure/loser", "I never do anything right", or
No one likes me". Know how to quickly identify these thoughts and counteract them!

Take a deep breath and try to clear your mind of clutter. Remind yourself that you are your hardest critic. Would you speak to your best friend that way? They're no reason you shouldn't be friends with yourself, and remembering to think positively about yourself is the first step. If you feel negativity creeping in, try to view the problem in a different light.

9). CHANGE YOUR MENTAL DIET

A very important aspect in having high self–esteem is first having a positive outlook on life. Whatever you choose to focus on – whether it's negative or positive –

expands and becomes more real. Whatever you put the most of your attention into will inevitably define your reality. So, here's where the big question comes in: Why would you choose to focus on something negative, when in the end, your life will become highly effected and ultimately defined by negativity? When it comes down to it, the concept is rather simple: if you want positive things to define your life, train your mind to view life with a positive outlook. A great way to stay positive is to focus on what makes you happier, and the goals you want to achieve. Reading uplifting books, and listening to uplifting music that puts you in a good mood are all great ways to keep your perspective on life positive.

And don't feel ashamed about the things that make you happy! Others may disregard them as childish or inferior to something else, but those people are only projecting their own insecurities on you. If listening to sappy pop music makes you happy, do it loudly and proudly! Maybe you feel better watching cartoons, or 80s sitcoms. Maybe you love romance novels. Find the things that makes you happy and stick to them. Don't let anyone shame you away from an activity you enjoy.

Sometimes, it can be therapeutic to re–visit the things you loved as a child. Regressing the mentality of a child is not good, but there's nothing wrong with re–watching a favorite cartoon or movie, listening to an album, or even purchase a toy from your childhood from the internet. Children's media, in particular, is focused on delivering important lessons while lessening the difficulties of the adult world. Escaping for a few hours may help you put your own problems in prospective, and revisiting something from your past may allow you to view things in a simpler way.

Sometimes it's helpful to unplug yourself from the rest of the world and focus on yourself. Turn off the news! Log off of social media! Put the phone on silent. Try to focus on positive feelings instead of the negative ones the media may stir. The world can be a bleak place, but there will always be a light that shines through that. Let yourself indulge in something uplifting. Look at pictures of baby animals or read positive news stories. Try to look at the world through a positive lens, even if it can be difficult.

Avoid negativity in your life by eliminating all of its sources. Stop watching the news! Avoid giving into the negativity–fueled drama of complainers and pessimists. Just walk away and don't look back!

10). DON'T MAKE YOUR PROBLEMS THE MAIN TOPIC OF YOUR CONVERSATIONS

This next one's important – don't make your problems the main topic of your conversations with people.

Instead of dwelling on all of the negative issues going on in your life and making them the centerpiece of your conversation, talk positively about your life, emphasizing on the progress you're trying to make in meeting your life priorities and achieving your goals. Always pay attention to how often you find yourself complaining or criticizing someone (this includes criticizing yourself), and find a way to be helpful instead of being critical and judgmental.

We all experiences various problems throughout the day that nag at us. Focusing every conversation you have on these issues will feeling draining and exhausting to your acquaintances. It's also critical to not focus on criticizing others. While it's natural to occasionally have an issue with an acquaintance or loved one, it's important to know the difference between sincere problems that need to be addressed and gossiping mean–spiritedly. It may make you temporarily feel better about yourself to critique how someone else looks, or how they act, but remember that this doesn't fix any of your problems and is often a reflection of your own low self–esteem. Try to be positive about yourself as well as other people, and take their feelings into consideration. Would ever want that person to know what you've said about them? If the answer is no, it's probably not something that needs to be said aloud.

It's also important to know your audience. You may complain more to your best friend than you should be a co-worker or the barista at the coffee shop. Oversharing, especially negative oversharing, can be daunting for other people who may not have the relationship with you they need to handle what you've told them. If you're having a bad day, you don't have to keep that to yourself, but make sure you're choosing the right time and venue to voice your complaints. And remember, it's important to listen just as much as you speak!

11). MAKE YOUR LIVING SPACE ORGANIZED AND ATTRACTIVE

Make your room and home/living space clean, organized, comfortable, and attractive. Display items like pictures, awards and creative work that you're proud of, to constantly remind you of your achievements, talents, and of special times and people in your life.

Wherever you live, whether it be a small apartment, a room with your parents, or a house, make sure that your space reflects your inner-self as best as possible. It's not realistic to think we can have show-room ready rooms all the time, or that we can all purchase expensive furniture, but sometimes all it takes is some cleaning, organization, and a little DIY to make a space feel comfortable. Not every space needs to be immaculate, but sprucing up a bit can do wonders for how you're feeling. Clean up any dirty plates or garbage, organize your belongings, and get rid of the clutter. If you find that your space doesn't reflect you, then try some simple steps to make it feel more homey. There are countless DIY projects you can do to make cool objects and decorations for any room. If you're on a budget, hit up the local thrift store for something you can use in your project, whether it's an old bust you spray paint your favorite color or a new wardrobe that needs minor repairs. Sometimes it takes something simple like a new bedspread or a few decorative pillows to really make a space feel alive.

12). DO SOMETHING NICE FOR YOURSELF

Pamper yourself every now and then – You deserve it! Treat yourself to a massage, a bath or nap. Take yourself out on a date. Treat yourself with the same respect, appreciation courtesy and kindness you would treat someone else – someone that you really, really liked. Feeling guilty defeats the purpose of this, because the whole point is to appreciate the experience! Treat yourself the way you want others to treat you.

Treat yourself to something every day, whether it's something small like an hour of your favorite television show or something more extravagant like a new pair of pants that make you feel great. It'll make hard days a little easier and good days that much more special. This goes back to the idea that you should treat yourself the way you'd want others to treat you. Being needlessly hard on yourself to be productive and frugal will not make you happy. Allowing yourself a moment of happiness every day will certainly send you in the right direction. When you treat yourself, acknowledge it. Thank yourself for being considerate.

13). PRACTICE MEDITATION

If you find yourself in a bad mood, feeling angry, low and anxious or lacking in self–confidence, the first step is to stop thinking, take some deep breaths. Some great ways to do this include exercising, involving yourself in something you enjoy that occupies your mind, and practicing meditation. Meditation is a fantastic life skill that allows you to relax yourself. Physical based relaxation techniques like Tai Chi are incredibly useful, as well.

Many people find yoga to be a stimulating way to go about meditation, as well. Anything that allows you to turn off your brain for a little while can be meditative and hugely restorative to a worried mind.

If you have ten minutes before bed or before you wake up, you can meditate. Start by finding a comfortable position. You can sit straight with your back against a wall, or lie down. Wherever you feel comfortable. Then, focus on breathing in and out slowly. Try to quiet the thoughts in your head. A big misconception about meditation is that you must completely quiet the mind to meditate successfully, but that is simply not true. The ideas that come buzzing through your head are natural. The trick is to let them pass and not linger on anything for too long. Let your worries slip in and out, and don't focus on anything but your breathing. If a thought seems to linger too long, re–align your thinking to focus on your body. Focus on breathing in and out slowly. Notice if your muscles are tensed or relaxed, and if they are tense, consciously force them into relaxation.

14). GET OTHERS INVOLVED IN A SUPPORT SYSTEM

Let your friends, family members and loved ones know what you are going through. You may be surprised to find they are willing to offer their support and advice. It's also a possibility that they are struggling with similar issues too, in which case you might be able to come together and form a support group.

If your family and friends are not very supportive. it may be helpful to look into your community for groups who may be able to help. Your local women's shelter may have some resources, or there may be support groups. By finding others who are feeling similarly, you may be able to make new friends and meaningful relationships.

15). BE A GOOD LISTENER

Whenever you find yourself interacting with someone, listen closely to the words they're saying and hear them out attentively. Try your hardest to develop the habit of understanding others, seeing things from different sides and perspectives, and acknowledging what they have to say. In the meantime, be sure to refrain from your own judgments and criticisms. BE A GOOD LISTENER – this is a very useful and important piece of advice to be applied no matter where you are, as being a good listener is one of the most respected and appreciated characteristics in a person.

When we're feeling down about ourselves, it can be easy to focus on our problems in conversation. Generally, we hope that discussing our feelings will help us feel better. However, it's important to realize that the people around you are often going through their own problems. Whether it's a co-worker or your best friend, taking a moment to sincerely ask how they are doing can do wonders to improve a relationship. When they're speaking about themselves, listen. If you find yourself queuing up your next response, stop. If the conversation begins to steer back toward you, ask a clarifying question. "How did you react?" or "How did you feel?" The person you're speaking to will likely be happy to elaborate, and by asking questions you appear attentive and thoughtful.

Remember, listening to others not only puts our lives in perspective, but works as a tool to better relationships. People always enjoy the company of a good listener.

16). CREATE AN EMPOWERING VISION

Using your imagination, create an empowering, positive image of yourself, in which you are the confident and self-assured person you aspire to become. When you imagine yourself as this person – this new and improved you, how will you feel? How will others view you? What will body language look like? How will you speak? Picture all of these things clearly in your mind's eye, keeping your eyes closed. Pay attention to the feelings, as you experience being and viewing things from that person's perspective. Now, make sure to practice this routinely, and do it for 10 minutes every morning. If you like, you can also play music in the background that either relaxes you, excites you, or puts you in a good mood. When you are done with this 10–minute exercise, jot down a detailed description of this person and all the attributes you've observed.

17). TAKE ACTION

Merely setting a goal alone won't get you any results, unless you're taking actions. Get clarity on your plans, and prepare a list of doable steps that you can take to achieve a goal. One of the most common reasons people get lazy and lose their motivation is because they don't have a strategy or plan to achieve their goals. They don't know where to start, what the next step is, or how to fully commit to their priorities, and instead start to wander off randomly. Take baking, for example: Imagine you're in the kitchen baking a cake. It's much easier to follow a set of clear, laid–out instructions, than randomly throwing ingredients together without a set plan.

18). DON'T ALWAYS WORRY ABOUT PLEASING OTHER PEOPLE

Don't constantly put yourself under the pressure of worrying about pleasing others. You are your own individual person, with your own set of unique needs, and you have the right to make your own decisions, think and choose for yourself, and your views and opinions are every bit as valid and important as anybody else's. Also, if you're constantly putting others people first and never thinking about yourself, or meeting your own needs, you'll end up being used – and not treated with the respect that you rightfully deserve

19). BE YOUR OWN PERSON

Don't try to emulate others and become a carbon copy of someone else – you are your own unique and special individual person. Instead of trying to change who you are, embrace every part of our personality, and remember that all of your quirks are the little things that make you, you!

Whether it's the media, our own inner–critic, or an outside voice, we are often told that if we just changed something crucial about ourselves our problems would melt away. There may be someone you greatly idolize who appears to have everything you want. In an attempt to mimic their success, you might adopt some of their habits. While this is okay to some degree (if you notice a powerful woman wearing beige high heels every time she has an important meeting, you might feel inclined to purchase some beige heels to feel empowered. Go for it!), it's important to stay true to yourself. Trying to mimic another person, or denying your true feelings for the sake of becoming someone else is an unhealthy, temporary fix for unhappiness. You're wonderful and unique on your own. Taking cues from others can be helpful and inspire us, but it's important to remember who you are. When in doubt, always opt to be genuine. You'll like your life better in the long run, and it'll amaze you to see the person you can become when you nurture yourself.

20). GAIN CLARITY – MAKE A PLAN

An effective way to boost self-esteem is getting prepared and organized – tying up those loose ends that make your life seem sloppy and disorganized (this contributes to low-self-esteem as it gives you the illusion that your life is chaotic and messy). Start by prioritizing and turning your focus towards on the life area that needs the most attention. Your self-esteem plays a very large, important role in all the major areas of your life. Start by writing down all of the major categories of your life, including your health, emotional stability, relationships, finance, etc. Once you've written everything down, rate yourself on a scale of 1–10 in each area. To help get you more organized, start working on the lowest numbered category first, and work your way up to the top. Each area influences and affects the other areas. The more you build up each area of your life, the more you'll improve all of the areas as a whole, which will result in an overall higher level of self-esteem and self-confidence.

21). TAKE RESPONSIBILITY FOR YOUR ACTIONS

Just like everyone is bound to inevitably make mistakes in their life, you will also, at some point or another in your life, intentionally or accidentally, disappoint and let others down. When that happens, and you find yourself in a situation where someone is upset with you for your actions, quit making excuses (notice how everyone seems to hate excuses?) and acknowledge the fact that you've made a mistake, while accepting it as a consequence of your choices. Instead of focusing on the regret, focus on what you can do to repair it.

Knowing when to say "I'm sorry" is a big indicator of confidence and maturity. Women are often taught that they should apologize for even minor inconveniences. Instead of saying, "I'm sorry, is this a good time?" when speaking to a co–worker or boss, just ask "Is this a good time?" Think about other similar instances in your life and eliminate the unneeded apology from your speech. You don't have to be apologetic for existing.

On the same hand, when you sincerely wrong a person or make a mistake, own up to it. Recognize that you've done something that has negatively affected someone or something. Learn from it. People respect those who can own up and take responsibility for their own mistakes instead of trying to pin it on others or make excuses for their mistakes. Be sure to put in genuine awareness by making an effort to fix things in a way that is beneficial to everyone involved. Sometimes, this can a lot of hard work, willpower, diligence and effort, but healthy self–esteem is rooted in knowing that you're someone who does the right thing.

22). HELP OTHERS FEEL GOOD ABOUT THEMSELVES, AS WELL

A great way to boost both your mood and your self-esteem is by helping somebody or teaching them something. When you help other people feel happier and better about themselves, it will in turn, also make you feel good about yourself. Think of ways you can make others feel good about themselves, or how you can make them smile. This can be done by giving them a kind and genuine compliment, teaching them something they'll be excited to learn, helping them with something, or telling them what you admire about them.

Often, women feel as though they're in competition with one another, which simply isn't true. Being catty due to jealousy, or to prove that you're the "better" woman is unnecessary and harmful. Instead, try to understand that other women have often faced similar struggles that you do. You may be jealous another woman got a promotion when you feel you should have, and it may make you feel better to think she used her sexuality to ascend. Try to stop yourself from doing this. Unless it's founded in truth, try to spin the situation into something positive. Likely, the other woman was more qualified for the job or was more vocal about her desire for the position. Instead of feeling envious, try to figure out a plan to do better next time.

Emily Hoskins

It's helpful to put aside envy and jealousy in favor of being supportive of other women. That doesn't mean you're obligated to like everyone you meet––that's impossible. Instead, try to understand their perspective. Many people face their own problems with self–esteem, and acting courteous toward everyone will not only win you respect from others, it will allow you to respect yourself.

No amount of money, fame, recognition, success, beauty, materialistic objects, intelligence, riches or strength can give you the same feeling of personal gratification, as well as the powerfully fulfilling sense of purpose as a genuine "thank you" from someone you help.

When you finally put an end to being consumed by your own worries, complaints, sorrows, negativity and melodrama, and instead, focus on ultimately being a part of the bigger picture – someone with a purpose to play in this universe, your sense of respect, self–esteem and self–value self–worth will get a highly improved, exponentially more meaningful, whole new definition. Be a giver, not just a taker, and give freely. Help someone whenever you see the opportunity. With the powerful sense of self-fulfillment that is achieved through actions of thoughtfulness and generosity, you will get more than what you thought you ever needed.

23). WHEN GREETING SOMEONE, SMILE AND MAKE DIRECT EYE CONTACT

Whenever you're greeting someone, make sure to smile and look them directly in the eye. Making direct eye contact with someone conveys confidence, which is a key element of self–respect.

Additionally, there are other ways to physically make yourself appear more confident. When you're walking, whether it be down the street or into a room, make sure your shoulders are squared and your back is straight. Your chin should be up. Speak slowly, making thoughtful pauses when you're gathering your thoughts. We often fill that space with "uhm" or some other filler word, when the reality is pausing gives us a moment to get on track while appearing thoughtful.

24). RESPOND TO PHONE CALLS PLEASANTLY

Be sure to always respond to phone calls pleasantly whether they're business phone calls or personal phone at home. It may seem silly, but smile when you answer the phone. Forcing yourself to smile will instantly cause your tone to be more pleasant. Be sure to give your name before asking to speak to whomever you're trying to reach. This is also a self–esteem booster, as it underscores that a person with self–respect is the one making the phone call.

On the subject of names, don't let others butcher yours. You may have an unusual name, or simply one unusual for the area that you live in. Don't let anyone mispronounce it. Correct them until they get it right. This is not rude or forceful, but rather shows that you are someone who deserves time and consideration.

25). ALWAYS SHOW APPRECIATION FOR GIFTS

Whenever someone gives you either a compliment or a gift, always make sure you show genuine appreciation to whomever it's coming from. Remember that you should always avoid downplaying expressions of affection or honor from others. A key attribute of an individual with high self–esteem is their ability to accept, as well as receive.

Acting flippant or uninterested in gifts will only make those who've given them to you feel like you're unappreciative or that you dislike what you've received. Even if that's the case (and who hasn't received a gift they don't want or like?) make sure to appreciate the act of giving a gift. It can feel awkward or even hurtful when someone gives a gift that doesn't suit you––almost as though the person doesn't know you well enough to know what you like––but some people are simply bad at picking out gifts. If an event is coming up and you're aware that someone is planning on giving you a gift, rather than dropping subtle hints (as we're often inclined to do), tell that person that you'd like a certain thing. Say something along the lines of, "I know my birthday is coming up and you're trying to figure out what to get me. I'd really like (blank) this year, if it's within your budget!" However, make sure to be aware of your audience. Asking your best friend who works for minimum wage to purchase you a hundred dollar gift is not going to go over well, or telling your husband who prides himself on picking out gifts for you what you'd like will likely hurt his feelings.

At the same time, try to be the kind of gift giver you would want to receive presents from. Be thoughtful of the recipient with each gift. If you know your sister loves orange but you hate that color and much prefer blue, don't opt to buy her a blue shirt just because you like it better. If you have a friend who appreciates sentiment much more than value or material items in a gift, make them a little gift basket of some kind or, if you're crafty, some sort of personalized gift. Being a good gift giver will not ensure that you will get the same treatment, but it will win you respect and admiration with others and show that you care about their interests and listen to what they say.

INSPIRATIONAL QUOTES ABOUT SELF ESTEEM:

"No one can make you feel inferior without your consent."

Former first lady and humanitarian Eleanor Roosevelt is attributed to that quote. Often, we find inspiration in words from others who have led successful lives. We may beat ourselves up over feeling like we've not achieved enough in life, or find ourselves too self–deprecating to get started. This can greatly affect self–esteem. Sometimes it's helpful to look to others and their words of encouragement for inspiration.

Here are several inspiring quotes by successful women that deal with self–esteem, success, opportunity, and confidence. These famous women include Maya Angelou, Gloria Steinam, Lucille Ball, Helen Keller and Oprah Winfrey.

"Far away there in the sunshine are my highest aspirations. I may not reach them, but I can look up and see their beauty, believe in them, and try to follow where they lead."– Louisa May Alcott, author of *Little Women*

"If you aren't good at loving yourself, you will have a difficult time loving anyone, since you'll resent the time and energy you give another person that you aren't even giving to yourself."– Barbara De Angelis, relationship consultant

"I began to understand that self–esteem isn't everything; it's just that there's nothing without it."– Gloria Steinem, feminist and political activist

"Our deepest fear is not that we are inadequate. Our deepest fear is that we are powerful beyond measure. It is our light, not our darkness that most frightens us. We ask ourselves, who am I to be brilliant, gorgeous, talented, fabulous? Actually, who are you not to be? You are a child of God. You're playing small does not serve the world. There is nothing enlightened about shrinking so that other people won't feel insecure around you. We are all meant to shine, as children do. We were born to make manifest the glory of God that is within us. It is not just in some of us; it is in everyone. And as we let our own light shine, we unconsciously give other people permission to do the same. As we are liberated from our own fear, our presence automatically liberates others."– Marianne Williamson, spiritual teacher

"Until you make peace with who you are, you'll never be content with what you have. – Doris Mortman, author

"I was once afraid of people saying, 'Who does she think she is?' Now I have the courage to stand and say, 'This is who I am'."–Oprah Winfrey, television personality and philanthropist

"Love yourself first and everything else falls into line. You really have to love yourself to get anything done in this world."– Lucille Ball, actress and television executive

"Remember always that you not only have the right to be an individual, you have an obligation to be one."– Eleanor Roosevelt, American politician and activist

"People may flatter themselves just as much by thinking that their faults are always present to other people's minds, as if they believe that the world is always contemplating their individual charms and virtues."– Elizabeth Gaskell, author

"Don't rely on someone else for your happiness and self–worth. Only you can be responsible for that. If you can't love and respect yourself – no one else will be able to make that happen. Accept who you are – completely; the good and the bad – and make changes as YOU see fit – not because you think someone else wants you to be different."– Stacey Charter, inspirational writer

"Never bend your head. Always hold it high. Look the world straight in the face."– Helen Keller, author and political activist

"You have been criticizing yourself for years, and it hasn't worked. Try approving of yourself and see what happens."– Louise L. Hay, motivational author

"The most beautiful people we have known are those who have known defeat, known suffering, known struggle, known loss, and have found their way out of the depths. These persons have an appreciation, a sensitivity and an understanding of life that fills them with compassions, gentleness, and a deep loving concern. Beautiful people do not just happen."– Elizabeth Kubler–Ross, psychiatrist

"You're always with yourself, so you might as well enjoy the company."– Diane Von Furstenberg, fashion designer

"The reward for conformity is that everyone likes you but yourself."– Rita Mae Brown, writer and feminist

"People are like stained–glass windows. They sparkle and shine when the sun is out, but when the darkness sets in their true beauty is revealed only if there is light from within."– Elisabeth Kübler–Ross, psychiatrist

"There came a time when the risk to remain tight in the bud was more painful than the risk it took to blossom."– Anaïs Nin, writer

"It took me a long time not to judge myself through someone else's eyes."– Sally Field, actress

"The most common way people give up their power is by thinking they don't have any."–Alice Walker, author

"I had to grow to love my body. I did not have a good self–image at first. Finally it occurred to me, I'm either going to love me or hate me. And I chose to love myself. Then everything kind of sprung from there. Things that I thought weren't attractive became sexy. Confidence makes you sexy."– Queen Latifah, actress and musician

"If you're presenting yourself with confidence, you can pull off pretty much anything." –Katy Perry, musician

"You only live once, but if you do it right, once is enough." — Mae West, actress

"Define success on your own terms, achieve it by your own rules, and build a life you're proud to live."–Anne Sweeney, co–chair of Disney

"I work really hard at trying to see the big picture and not getting stuck in ego. I believe we're all put on this planet for a purpose, and we all have a different purpose... When you connect with that love and that compassion, that's when everything unfolds."– Ellen DeGeneres, comedian

"I've learned that people will forget what you said, people will forget what you did, but people will never forget how you made them feel."– Maya Angelou, author

"I don't believe in guilt, I believe in living on impulse as long as you never intentionally hurt another person, and don't judge people in your life. I think you should live completely free." – Angelina Jolie, actress and humanitarian

"I believe in pink. I believe that laughing is the best calorie burner. I believe in kissing, kissing a lot. I believe in being strong when everything seems to be going wrong. I believe that happy girls are the prettiest girls. I believe that tomorrow is another day and I believe in miracles."–Audrey Hepburn, actress

"You may not always have a comfortable life and you will not always be able to solve all of the world's problems at once but don't ever underestimate the importance you can have because history has shown us that courage can be contagious and hope can take on a life of its own."– Michelle Obama, first lady of the United States

"We need to accept that we won't always make the right decisions, that we'll screw up royally sometimes – understanding that failure is not the opposite of success, it's part of success."–Arianna Huffington, co–founder *Huffington Post*

"My will shall shape the future. Whether I fail or succeed shall be no one's doing but my own. I am the force. I can clear any obstacle before me or I can be lost in the maze. My choice. My responsibility. Win or lose; only I hold the key to my destiny."—Elaine Maxwell, professional kickboxer and MMA fighter

"When someone tells me 'no', it doesn't mean I can't do it, it simply means I can't do it with them."—<u>Karen E. Quinones Miller</u>, journalist and historian

"Destiny is a name often given in retrospect to choices that had dramatic consequences."—J. K. Rowling, author

"Success is most often achieved by those who don't know that failure is inevitable." — <u>Coco Chanel</u>, fashion designer

"Never dull your shine for somebody else." — <u>Tyra Banks</u>, supermodel and entrepreneur

"Life is not easy for any of us. But what of that? We must have perseverance and above all confidence in ourselves. We must believe that we are gifted for something and that this thing must be attained." — Marie Curie, scientist

"So many people are shut up tight inside themselves like boxes, yet they would open up, unfolding quite wonderfully, if only you were interested in them."— Sylvia Plath, poet

"I always thought that people told you that you're beautiful––that this was a title that was bestowed upon you…I think that it's time to take this power into our own hands and to say, 'You know what? I'm beautiful. I just am. And that's my light. I'm just a beautiful woman'."—Margaret Cho, comedian

"I believe with all my heart that the cliches are true, that we are our own best friends and best company, and that if you're not right for yourself, it's impossible to be right for anyone."— Rachel Machacek, writer

"Life can take so many twists and turns. You can't ever count yourself out. Even if you're really afraid at some point, you can't think that there's no room for you to grow and do something good with your life."— Portia de Rossi, actress

"Trying to build myself up with the fact that I have done things right that were even good and have had moments that were excellent but the bad is heavier to carry around and feel have no confidence."— Marilyn Monroe, model and actress

"Happiness and confidence are the prettiest things you can wear"—<u>Taylor Swift</u>, musician

"You are more powerful than you know; you are beautiful just as you are."—Melissa Etheridge, musician

"I always did something I was a little not ready to do. I think that's how you grow. When there's that moment of 'Wow, I'm not really sure I can do this,' and you push through those moments, that's when you have a breakthrough."—Marissa Mayer, CEO of Yahoo

"When I'm not feeling my best I ask myself, 'What are you gonna do about it?' I use the negativity to fuel the transformation into a better me." –Beyonce Knowles, musician

"Have a go-to pump up song. Mind is Shakira's 'Waka Waka' from the 2010 World Cup (don't judge). Play it only when you're ready to turn into your most badass self." –Kathryn Minshew, founder and CEO, themuse.com

"Think like a queen. A queen is not afraid to fail. Failure is another stepping stone to greatness." –Oprah Winfrey

"Just believe in yourself. Even if you don't, pretend that you do and, at some point, you will." –Venus Williams, tennis champion

"I always did something I was a little not ready to do. I think that's how you grow. When there's that moment of 'Wow, I'm not really sure I can do this', and you push through those moments, that's when you have a breakthrough. Sometimes that's a sign that something really good is about to happen. You're about to grow and learn a lot about yourself." —Marissa Mayer, CEO of Yahoo

"But that inadequacy, or feeling of inadequacy, never really goes away. You just have to trudge ahead in the rain, regardless." —<u>Lorrie Moore</u>, fiction writer

Emily Hoskins

Chapter 7
Stop Falling Into the Comparison Trap

As women, we often put ourselves under an immense amount of pressure to be the "ideal woman". We often fall into the trap of comparing ourselves to other women, and holding a secret competition with them. This results in jealously, which in turn can lead to plummeted self–esteem.

No one's life is perfect. The sitcom-perfect family next door may have tremendous debt. The successful may battle with alcoholism. The handsome couple you see walking down the street might be on the verge of breaking-up. It's difficult to judge a book by its cover, and many people put on a front to make it look like they have their life together. It truth, their lives are just as chaotic and uncertain as yours. Everyone experiences the ups and downs, and it's possible for anyone to get stuck in the down stage. Don't beat yourself up for not comparing to the imaginary lives of others. Likely, you're doing just fine, and there's certainly someone who finds your life or looks enviable. Instead of constantly comparing yourselves to others, try to find the positives in your own life. Appreciate what you have, and if you want to change something, make sure it's because you want to, not because you're trying to keep up with the Joneses.

DON'T JUDGE A BOOK BY ITS COVER

Just because your neighbor – let's call her "Lucy"– seems to have everything you could have ever dreamed of (the perfect body, perfect husband, perfect home, and perfect family) doesn't mean her life is as perfect as it seems. Even though people's lives often seem a certain way, it is important not to judge their inner life based on its outer appearance – you don't know what type of personal struggles they are dealing with behind closed doors. For example, the owner of that beautiful house may have a crippling illness that you don't know about. The seemingly perfect couple may have relationship issues, or financial difficulties you aren't aware of. We are all fighting our own battles in life, and there is no such thing as a "perfect human", no matter how perfect they may appear on the outside. Life is also far too short to fall into the comparison trap – in the end, none of it will matter.

I, myself have had a personal experience that led me into viewing people in a complete different manner. When I was in high school, I constantly would find myself being a jealous, green–eyed monster, whether it was of other girls' looks, name–brand clothes, boyfriends, and body–type. There was one girl in particular, whom I always envied. She was absolutely gorgeous! With her long blonde hair, model–like body, deep blue eyes and flawless complexion, I only wished I could be her. If only I was in her shoes, my life would be perfect, I thought to myself. However, years later, I found out that she had been battling leukemia, and had just passed away. This made me stop comparing myself to other women, because you never know what personal struggles they suffer from in their own life. It's important to live and let live – this will also help you have a higher self–esteem, as well as a more positive, empathetic outlook on life, and on others.

LIFE IS TOO SHORT FOR LETTING YOURSELF FALL INTO THE COMPARISON TRAP!

Emily Hoskins

Chapter 8
How to Boost Your Self–Confidence

"Once we believe in ourselves, we can risk curiosity, wonder, spontaneous delight, or any experience that reveals the human spirit."
– E.E. Cummings

A great way to boost your self–esteem is by being confident in yourself. One of the things that would always hold me back in life was my fear of failure, and my lack of confidence to overcome this fear. It's nearly impossible to break free from your traditional mold, go after your dreams and truly be yourself if you have low–confidence. By working on building up my confidence and self–esteem, I was able to slowly but surely overcome these fears, and finally accomplish the things I always had wanted to in life.

Self-esteem and self-confidence are closely connected to each other. Having self-confidence means you believe in yourself. Having high self-esteem is believing you are worthy of respect from others. You can think of self-confidence as a crucial stepping stone to building high self-esteem.

To achieve a goal, which in this case is developing confidence and ultimately achieving high self-esteem, it's important to start working towards this goal with small, doable steps. If you believe that you aren't competent, attractive or smart, this can certainly be changed. Here are several things you can do that will help boost your confidence and raise your self-esteem:

1). MENTALLY PHOTOSHOP YOUR SELF-IMAGE

This particular method has significantly helped me boost my self-confidence. Your self-image is the way you picture yourself in your own mind. This mental picture determines how confident we are in ourselves. We each have the capacity to change how we view ourselves. Think of your mind as a computer, and as such, it comes equipped with photoshop. If your self-image isn't good, use your mental photoshopping skills to make it better! Replace the negative qualities with positive qualities you have, and think to yourself, "I am worth it!"

While this can refer to how you physically see yourself, it should be broadened to include the whole picture of how you see yourself. If you see yourself as worthless, try to photoshop that away! You're a worthwhile person, even if you find it hard to believe sometimes. You bring something valuable to the world, and believing in yourself will allow you to share this. No matter where you've come from or where you are, you've worked hard to get this far. The hardest thing anyone can do is live, and you deserve to acknowledge this accomplishment. Let your self-image reflect this. You're a warrior, a fighter, and most importantly, a survivor.

We each have the capacity to change how we view ourselves. Think of your mind as a computer, and as such, it comes equipped with photoshop.

2). GROOM YOURSELF

This may seem like an obvious one, but it's amazing how much better you can feel after taking a simple shower! Sometimes when I'm in the shower, I picture it as a therapeutic way of cleansing myself of "impurities", so to speak. These impurities include low self–confidence as well as self–doubt. You'll be surprised at the amazing difference that a shower and a shave can make in your feelings of self–confidence and self-image.

While it's necessary to keep up basic upkeep, treat yourself to a relaxing at-home spa treatmnet. This can mean a multitude of things, depending on your own cleanliness standards. Do whatever makes you feel like a million bucks. Take an hour to give yourself a manicure or pedicure. Whip up a quick face mask. Massage your scalp while in the shower. Clear your pores with a steam-based facial. Whiten your teeth. Try new make-up techniques. Try a new soothing lotion. Maintain body hair. Whatever it is, make sure it makes you feel good about yourself. While you're at it, brew yourself a herbal tea or drink water with lemon. When you treat yourself like a movie star, you'll fell like one. This can be particularly efficient as a pick-me-up when you aren't feeling great about yourself.

Showering every day or every other day is necessary to maintain basic cleanliness. However, it can also function as an important intimate moment with your body each day. Is there any time we're more vulnerable then when we're naked? Many women feel uncomfortable looking at their naked body and avoid it at all costs. It's important to come to terms with the fact that avoiding your body will not make it thinner, younger, or curvier. Ignoring it will only feed into any negative feelings you have about it. If you typically avoid looking at yourself in the mirror, stop. Take a moment to acknowledge what your body looks like. Remind yourself that you're beautiful and there's nothing wrong or unusual about your body. It may feel forced at first, but over time you will begin to believe it. This can also apply in the shower, when you might avoid looking at your belly, thighs, or other body part. Don't give into your desire to look away. It's better to confront your insecurity than ignore it. Your body, whatever it looks like, is nothing to be ashamed of.

3). REMOVE TOXIC PEOPLE FROM YOUR LIFE

Is there a bully in your life that is making it increasingly difficult for you to have high self-esteem by constantly dragging you down and convincing you that you're not worth it? Removing "toxic people" from your life will remove the negativity that is dragging you down and preventing you from believing in yourself and living your life to the fullest.

4). DRESS NICELY

If you dress nicely, you will feel good about yourself. You will feel successful, presentable and ready to get out there, accomplish the things you've been putting off, and tackle the world! Now, by telling you to dress nicely,

I'm not suggesting for you to hit the upscale boutiques and purchase ridiculously expensive outfits – dressing nicely can mean wearing casual, neat–looking and presentable clothing.

On occasion, the best medicine is obtaining a new outfit that makes you feel sexy and confident. If you have the expendable funds, it can be nice to treat yourself to new clothes. However, there are other options if you don't have a lot of money for frivolous spending. Find yourself some new thrift store duds. You can host a body positive clothing exchange with some friends. Or you can even take some of your old clothing and transform it with a DIY project. Whatever it is, find a way to express yourself in your clothing and look the way that makes you feel good!

5) THINK POSITIVE

This may seem like a corny phrase that is used far too often, but thinking positive thoughts definitely improves entire situations! When you think positively, you are letting the universe know that you welcome positivity, which in turn signals more positive outcomes in your life! For example, when I first started drawing, I replaced the negative thoughts and fear of failure with positive thoughts. With this tiny skill, I was able to improve my drawing skills significantly, and now have a thick 100–page drawing pad filled with many professional–looking drawings!

If you enjoy doing something, try not to worry about what other people think of it. It may take you a while to practice and improve a new skill, but persisting will only allow you to get better. Silence the nay-sayers. As mentioned in another chapter, those who criticize your early efforts to learn a skill are generally toxic individuals battling their own insecurities. As a result, they're reflecting those self-esteem issues onto you. Don't let them succeed.

6). ACT POSITIVE

In addition to thinking positive thoughts, you must also be positive in your actions. This is actually the key to developing self–confidence. You are what you do, and if you change what you do, you change what you are. Instead of negatively thinking to yourself that you can't accomplish something, take action in a positive way. This will significantly help you develop self–confidence and high self–esteem!

If, for instance, you use social media, try not to update every time something negative happens to you. It's draining on others and comes off as a bad reflection of who you are as a person. Constant complaining online can feel whiny to others, and get old fast. People will think you're a natural pessimist. That may be true, but the internet is already filled with bad news. While it's okay, and even sometimes humorous or necessary, to bring up negative events via social media once in a while, try to fill your space on the internet with positivity. The internet can be an incredibly negative place sometimes, and people will appreciate that you're not continuously contributing. Others aside, posting about every bad thing that happens throughout the day can have a harmful impact on your own mental health. It can be difficult to see others celebrate accomplishments while it seems like you can never get ahead. Filling your space with positive or humorous notes about your day can serve as a helpful reminder that your life has its own special moments.

7). BE KIND AND THOUGHTFUL TO OTHERS

Being kind, thoughtful and giving to others is a wonderful way to boost self-confidence because you will see yourself as a good person, and so will others! No, you don't have to spend a fortune on buying extravagant gifts to make this happen. Being thoughtful and giving can be as simple as baking cookies for family members, or offering your significant other a back massage when you hear them complaining about back-pains. A thoughtful and kind person is respected and appreciated by everyone!

8). SPEAK SLOWY

This is probably the simplest thing on this entire list, but can make an incredibly significant difference in how others perceive you. A person with authority speaks slowly, because they are confident about what they have to say. A person with low-confidence feels like they aren't worth listening to, therefore will speak quickly because they do not want to keep people waiting on something that isn't worth listening to. Speaking slowly immediately puts you in an authoritative position and lets people know that you're confident, and worth listening carefully to. Of course, don't take it to an extreme, but avoiding sounding rushed when you speak. Speaking in a rushed tone also causes people to interrupt you more often, but a slower way of speaking tends to cause people to shut up and pay attention to what you have to say. Slower talking = more confidence!

Implementing these confidence-boosting steps into your daily life will undoubtedly improve the way you feel about yourself, as well as the way others perceive and treat you. The result? Heightened confidence and improved self-esteem!

Emily Hoskins

Chapter 9
How Practicing Meditation Helps Build Self–Esteem

Meditation is an amazingly effective way to build your self–esteem. In addition, it significantly improves every aspect your physical and emotional health. Many meditation techniques are very helpful, as they involve eliminating every thought that's going through your head. Clearing your mind by getting rid of negative thoughts will help restart your mind and allow it to be more relaxed, which will allow you to think more clearly and rationally.

As mentioned earlier in the book, it's important to remember that negative thoughts that filter through during meditation are not abnormal and it doesn't mean that you're meditating wrong! Instead, focus on not engaging with those thoughts. Instead of allowing anxiety, criticisms, and worries to have any space in your head, simply let those thoughts pass. If you find yourself too fixated on something to meditate, try to refocus your mind onto your breathing. Focus on the way breathing forces your chest to expand and collapse. Notice how you physically feel doing the meditation. Don't let negativity invade this space for long!

Practicing mindfulness meditation techniques has been shown to have a wide variety of incredible benefits for your overall health and well-being! It has the power to improve all aspects of your physical and emotional health, benefitting you as a whole. Here are some excellent reasons as to why should start practicing mindfulness meditation today! Meditation has been shown to reduce chronic pain, lower blood pressure, and alleviate a wide array of gastrointestinal issues.

It also improves sleep, decreases insomnia, helps treat heart disease, and stress. Mindfulness meditation also improves an array of mental/emotional aspects of your health. For instance, it helps treat depression, reduce obsessive compulsive behaviors, anxiety, relationship conflicts, stress and irritability and negative thought patterns associated with eating disorders. It also acts as an important element in treating substance abuse.

Meditation has also been shown to increase brain function, as well as the grey matter that is found in areas of the brain associated with self–awareness, empathy, self–control and attention. Another favorable brain–benefit of meditation is that it has also been proven to regulate the part of the brain that produces stress hormones (cortisol), which in turn reduces stress.

Mindfulness meditation has many favorable advantages that lead to a plethora of improvements and enhancements in virtually every aspect of your physical and emotional health. It has the incredible power to improve immunity while creating positive brain changes, lower stress, and assist in coping with chronic health issues such as chronic pain, cancer and heart disease, only to name a few. A recent meta–analysis of 20 empirical reports has shown plenty of evidence that mindfulness meditation drastically increased both physical and mental well–being in patients who were battling with heart disease, chronic pain, cancer and autoimmune disorders.

Researchers at the University of Oregon have found that participating in integrative–body–mind–training, a highly effective mindfulness meditation technique, actually causes positive brain changes and enhancements that actually protect our brains against a wide array of mental illnesses! In addition, integrative–

body–mind–training has also shown to be linked with improved axonal density, which are the signaling connections in our brain. This handy little meditation technique also leads to an increased amount of protective tissue, or myelin, around the axons in the anterior cingulate brain region.

Many experts believe that one of the prominently important ways that mindfulness meditation works is by improving peoples' ability to accept their experiences — including painful and unpleasant emotions that are associated with difficult experiences and situations — rather than immediately react to them negatively with resentment, fear, anger, bitterness, aversion and avoidance. The wonderful thing about practicing mindfulness meditation is that it heals and improves our mental/emotional state by causing us to view life in a much clearer, wiser, more rational and healthier perspective.

It's actually becoming more and more common for mindfulness meditation to be combined with psychotherapy, particularly cognitive behavioral therapy. This development in psychotherapy makes clear and perfect sense, as meditation and cognitive behavioral therapy both share the same goal of helping people gain awareness, understanding and a better perspective on maladaptive, destructive, irrational and self–defeating thought patterns.

Meditation Helps You Become a Better Person – Literally!

According to a study in the journal, Psychological Science, mindfulness has a virtuous effect on us, causing us to be more compassionate, which benefits the people who we interact with! In addition, researchers from Harvard and Northwestern Universities discovered that meditation, particularly mindfulness, is actually very strongly linked with increased patterns of more virtuous, "do–good" behavior. Who would've thought!

Meditation Helps Support Weight–Loss!

In a recent Women's Health study that was conducted at Harvard Medical School, participants who practiced mindful eating (they ate slowly, while savoring the food and paying attention to the sensations they felt with each bite) consumed a significantly reduced the amount of caloric intake than those who didn't engage in mindful eating, even though they were hungrier than the opposing control groups! This led the mindful–eaters to lose more weight in the long run, as well as a newly gained appreciation for healthier foods. This will also lead to developed long–term healthy eating–

patterns, which helps maintain healthy weight in the long run.

BREATHING MEDITATION:

Begin by finding a quiet, peaceful and distraction–free place. Now with your back straight. Relax, focus and feel each sensation that comes with each breath you take as it slowly moves in and out of your body. Let your distracting thoughts of everything else disappear, and just direct your focus on breathing. Pay attention to your nostrils as the air moves in and out. Notice how your abdomen expands and then collapses with each breath. When your mind begins to wander, stop and gently redirect your undivided attention to your breath. Don't judge yourself. Keep in mind that you're not trying to beat or master anything — such as becoming a skilled meditator, as this isn't a race to perfection. You're simply eliminating all of your thoughts and instead, becoming in touch and aware of all of the simple little details involved in what's happening around you, breath by breath.

PROGRESSIVE MUSCLE RELAXATION MEDITATION TECHNIQUE

Before practicing this exercise, make sure you first consult with your doctor if you suffer from any physical complications including muscle spasms, back or neck problems, or other injuries or muscle conditions that can be potentially aggravated by tensing your muscles.

Start by getting totally comfortable – remove your shoes and change into comfortable clothing. Now that you're dressed comfortably, take a few minutes to just relax and take nice and slow deep breaths. Inhale and exhale.

When you feel like you're relaxed enough and are ready to start with the exercise, direct all of your undivided attention to your right foot. Take a few silent, peaceful moments to focus on how it feels, and be aware of every sensation.

Next, start to slowly tense your right–foot muscles, while squeezing as tightly as you possibly can. Do this for 10 seconds – If you like, you can count to 10 out loud. Now move onto your right foot, relax and direct your full focus on the tension that's flowing away from your foot, and how it feels as it becomes relaxed.

Stay in this peaceful and relaxed state for a few moments, while slowly and calmly taking deep breaths.

Inhale and exhale. When you're ready to move on, direct your entire focus onto your left foot. Now repeat the same process of the muscle tension and release, the same way you did on your right foot. Move slowly upwards throughout your whole body, contracting and relaxing the various muscle groups as you go. It may take some practice and discipline at first, but try not to tense your muscles for longer than 10 seconds.

WALKING MEDITATION

This incredibly healthy practice works wonders on clearing your mind and helping you cope with overwhelming emotions, including grief. For this exercise, start by first finding a space outside, and simply begin walking at slow to medium pace, while focusing on your feet. Try to pay close attention to when your toes touch the ground, when your foot is flat and pressing against the ground and when your toe points back in an upward position. Now, feel the roll of your foot, paying close attention to every sensation, and noticing each sensory detail – whether you feel a tingle, a pull of the sock there, and how your foot feels against the ground.

When feel your mind beginning to wander into the chaotic land of scattered thoughts, which it probably will (and it's completely normal), shut off your mind and gently proceed to bring your attention back to your feet after you've eliminated all other thoughts. With this exercise, you're practicing and building the important skill of being aware when your concentration begins drifting into default mode. At the same time, you'll also be training yourself to bring it back into focus. Building and strengthening this skill will effectively help you be more present in the moment, and more in control of your thoughts and attention, every day, and will be particularly useful in times of stress when our minds tend to wander most. With the skill, you'll be more in touch with your thought patterns, while knowing what your brains up to. This will help you immediately identify the negative thought patterns associated with low self–esteem, that way you can put a stop to them and shift to a more positive place in your mind.

For this exercise, it can be very helpful and rewarding to dedicate a specific time and chosen location to practice. When you have become more comfortable with walking meditation, try taking it to the next level by practicing as you're walking to the bus stop, office, classroom, grocery store or just about anywhere you please.

Not only will engaging mindful–meditation techniques virtually benefit all aspects of your body, both physically and emotionally, it will also offer favorable benefits and improvements to every aspect of your life, including relationships, family situations and work. It will also allow you to view each situation and aspect in your life with a positive perspective. You will realize the positive benefits they offer, rather than the stress, negativity and inconvenience.

Conclusion

Although low self-esteem may seem like a hopelessly permanent thought pattern in which you will always remain molded into, IT'S NOT! By following the various helpful steps and strategies that were mentioned in this book, you will be well on your way to achieve unbreakable confidence, self-love and high self-esteem.

The next time you find yourself discouraged at the aspects in your life you wish were different, begin to think positively, and follow by continuously applying the advice that was mentioned in this book. This will result in far better outcomes in various different aspects of your life, as well a significantly happier you.

ALWAYS REMEMBER: YOU ARE WORTH IT!

Emily Hoskins